DATE DUE

GAYLORD			PRINTED IN U.S.A.

Taking Responsibility

by Stuart Schwartz and Craig Conley

Content Consultant:
Robert J. Miller, Ph.D.
Associate Professor
Mankato State University

C A P S T O N E
H I G H / L O W   B O O K S
an imprint of Capstone Press

C A P S T O N E   P R E S S

818 North Willow Street • Mankato, MN 56001
http://www.capstone-press.com

Library of Congress Cataloging-in-Publication Data
Schwartz, Stuart, 1945-
     Taking responsibility/by Stuart Schwartz and Craig Conley.
     p. cm. -- (Job skills)
     Includes bibliographical references and index.
     Summary: Explains how to perform responsibly and assume responsibility in
the workplace.
     ISBN 1-56065-717-0
     1. Career development--Juvenile literature. 2. Work ethic--Juvenile literature.
3. Job satisfaction--Juvenile literature. [1. Career development. 2. Work ethic. 3. Job
satisfaction.] I. Conley, Craig, 1965- . II. Title. III. Series: Schwartz, Stuart, 1945-
Job skills.
HF5381.S2864 1998
650.1--dc21   97-53219
                                                                          CIP
                                                                          AC

Photo credits:
All photos by Dede Smith Photography

Table of Contents

Inspected by

Erik & La

Chapter 1

Why Take Responsibility?

People must be responsible when they take jobs. Responsible means being trustworthy and dependable. Employers prefer to hire people who are responsible. An employer is a person or company that hires and pays workers. Employers know they can count on responsible workers. Responsible workers perform their jobs well.

Being responsible can also help workers. Employers often give raises to responsible workers. A raise is an increase in pay. For example, a responsible sales clerk who does a good job each day may receive a raise.

Responsible workers also receive promotions. A promotion is a better or higher-paying job. For example, an employer might promote a responsible sales clerk to supervisor. A supervisor is a person who is in charge of workers.

Being responsible takes many skills. It means more than just doing a job.

Responsible workers do jobs well.

Your Employee
Handbook

Chapter 2

Doing Good Work

A worker's most important responsibility is doing the job well. The first step is understanding the job. Workers must know what employers expect them to do.

Many jobs have written job descriptions. A job description is a list of duties. It may also include other information that the worker should know.

Responsible workers know their job duties. For example, a nurse takes care of sick people. The nurse knows one duty is to give medicine. Another duty is taking patients' temperatures.

Sometimes it takes time to learn duties. Responsible workers take the time to learn their duties. They ask their supervisors questions. They ask other workers for help. For example, an office worker might ask how to fix a computer problem. A food server might ask how to carry trays without spilling them.

Responsible workers know all of their duties. They try hard to perform their duties. They do the best jobs they can.

Many jobs have written job descriptions.

Chapter 3

Completing Tasks

Each job includes many tasks. Workers are responsible for completing these tasks. For example, a receptionist's main task is to answer phones. But a receptionist must also take messages and direct calls to the right workers.

Responsible workers have plans for completing their tasks. They think about which tasks are most important. If they are not sure, workers ask their supervisors which tasks are most important. For example, a baker does not know what to bake first. The baker asks a supervisor. The supervisor says wheat bread sells best. The baker decides to bake wheat bread first.

Many workers list their tasks. They write when each task must be done. This helps them finish tasks on time. It helps them be responsible.

Sometimes finishing tasks is hard. A factory worker might put together car parts. A machine breaks down. The worker cannot finish the task. A responsible worker looks for other tasks to do until the machine is fixed. The worker may even help fix the machine.

Each job includes many tasks.

Chapter — 4

Reaching Goals

Responsible workers try to reach goals. A goal is an objective people try to accomplish.

It is not easy to reach goals. It can take a long time to reach big goals. Some people set many small goals. These goals can be steps to reaching one big goal.

For example, a supervisor might ask a worker to pack 50 boxes per day. The worker packs 35 boxes on the first day. The next day, the worker finds ways to work faster. The worker packs 40 boxes. The worker keeps trying. After a week, the worker reaches the goal of 50 per day.

Reaching goals takes perseverance. Perseverance is the ability to keep trying despite problems. The worker could have given up. Instead, the worker kept trying. The worker reached the goal by acting responsibly.

Responsible workers try to reach goals.

Chapter — 5

Standards and Details

Responsible workers have high standards for themselves. A standard is a measure of quality. Setting high standards means expecting high quality.

For example, responsible nurses set high standards. Nurses give sick people their medicine. One mistake could hurt a sick person. Responsible nurses try not to make any mistakes. Their standards are very high.

Workers with high standards pay attention to details. Details are the small but important parts of a job. Doing a good job means paying attention to details. One small mistake can ruin a whole task.

For example, workers at fast food restaurants check each order. They make sure orders are correct. One mistake means an order is wrong. Wrong orders make customers unhappy. Good workers take responsibility for the details of their jobs. If they do make mistakes, they try to correct them.

Workers with high standards pay attention to details.

Chapter 6

Concentration

Good workers pay careful attention to their work. This is called concentration. Concentration helps workers do jobs quickly, correctly, and safely.

Good workers keep their minds on their work. They chat with others only at break time. Workers who concentrate on their jobs get more work done.

Concentration leads to better work. For example, an office worker listens to the radio while typing a memo. This keeps the worker from concentrating. The worker makes several errors and must retype the memo. The worker turns the radio off. The worker can concentrate better on typing the memo when the radio is off.

Concentration also makes a workplace safer. For example, a factory worker uses a machine to cut paper. The machine could also cut the worker's hands. The worker must pay close attention when operating the machine. Workers who concentrate are safer on the job.

Good workers concentrate on their work.

Chapter 7

Attendance and Punctuality

Workers depend on each other. If someone misses work, other workers have to do more work. The other workers may also fall behind in their own work.

For example, a child care worker decides to stay home one day. The worker does not tell the supervisor. The other workers must care for more children. Their jobs become harder. Missing work for unimportant reasons is not fair to other workers. It is not responsible.

Responsible workers only miss work for very good reasons. They might miss work if they are sick or if there is an emergency. An emergency is a sudden and risky situation. They may plan ahead to take some days off. This is called vacation.

Responsible workers arrive at work on time. Arriving on time is called punctuality. Punctuality shows that workers care about their jobs. Other workers can depend on them. Workers who are not punctual can lose their jobs. Those who miss too much work may also lose their jobs.

Responsible workers arrive at work on time.

Chapter 8

Following Rules and Directions

Every employer has rules. Responsible workers follow their employers' rules. Employers' rules are meant to help workers perform their duties. Some rules are written down. Some rules are spoken. Responsible workers know and follow all the rules. Following rules helps keep workers safe.

For example, welders use heat to join pieces of metal. The pieces of metal often give off sparks. Welders must wear special glasses when welding. The glasses protect their eyes from sparks. Workers who follow this rule are safer.

Responsible workers also follow directions. Directions are the steps necessary to complete tasks. Cooks follow directions when preparing meals. They know that the food tastes better when they follow directions.

Responsible workers follow directions.

Chapter 9

Improving Skills

Every job takes certain skills. Improving skills helps workers do a better job. Employers value skilled workers.

Workers improve their skills by learning. For example, mechanics might improve their skills by learning new ways to use tools. Teachers might improve their skills by studying how people learn.

Responsible workers look for ways to improve their skills. For example, an employer might decide to buy a computer system. Responsible workers would take classes and learn how to use computers.

Some employers offer classes to teach new skills. Workers can take classes at schools and colleges. Workers can also learn more by reading books or magazines about their jobs. For example, a cook can read magazines about food preparation. A teacher can read about new teaching methods.

Meetings with other workers can be helpful, too. Workers can share ideas about how they do their jobs.

Workers can take classes to learn new job skills.

Chapter 10

Having a Positive Attitude

Good workers have positive attitudes. They are enthusiastic about their work. Enthusiastic means excited and interested. A positive attitude shows workers care about their work.

Employers value workers with positive attitudes. For example, a salesperson might sell newspapers and magazines. The salesperson has a positive attitude. The salesperson helps people find the magazines they want. A supervisor sees that the salesperson cares about the job. The salesperson might get a raise.

Having a positive attitude also helps workers learn new skills. Sometimes workers make mistakes. But workers with positive attitudes keep trying. They know that making mistakes is part of learning.

For example, a florist sells flowers. The florist might send someone the wrong flowers. The mistake costs money. But the florist has a positive attitude. The florist learns what caused the mistake and sends the right flowers.

Having a positive attitude helps workers.

Chapter 11

Energy on the Job

Work takes energy. Good workers are energetic. Energetic workers are enthusiastic. They work hard. They keep going until jobs are done. Employers can count on energetic workers to do their jobs.

Workers who lack energy may not be able to concentrate. They may work slowly or make mistakes. For example, a tailor sews clothes. The tailor stays up late one night. In the morning, the tailor skips breakfast. At work, the tailor makes four dresses too short. Other tailors have to fix the dresses.

Workers can do several things to maintain their energy. They can eat healthy foods for breakfast, lunch, and dinner. They can stretch or take short walks during breaks to renew their energy. They can get the right amount of sleep at night. Workers who eat and sleep poorly often lack energy on the job.

Energetic workers keep going until jobs are done.

Chapter — 12

Responsibility and You

Responsible workers understand and care about their jobs. They know what their employers expect of them. They come to work on time every day. They have high standards. Responsible workers know and follow the rules.

Being responsible means more than just getting the job done. You can improve your skills. You can take classes or learn more about your job by reading. You can bring a positive attitude to your place of work. You can make choices that help you maintain your energy.

Thinking about responsibility can help you do a better job. Acting responsibly shows your employer that you take the job seriously. Being responsible will help you be a success.

Responsible workers bring positive attitudes to work.

Words to Know

concentration (kon-suhn-TRAY-shuhn)— paying careful attention

details (DEE-taylz)—the small but important parts of a job

directions (duh-REK-shuhnz)—the steps necessary to complete tasks

employer (em-PLOI-ur)—a person or company that hires and pays workers

enthusiastic (en-thoo-zee-ASS-tik)—excited and interested

job description (JOB di-SKRIP-shuhn)—a list of duties

perseverance (pur-suh-VEER-uhnss)—the ability to keep trying despite problems

promotion (pruh-MOH-shun)—a better or higher-paying job

punctuality (puhngk-choo-AL-i-tee)—being on time

To Learn More

Goley, Elaine P. *Learn the Value of Responsibility*. Vero Beach, Fla.: Rourke Enterprises, 1988.

Hawk, Barbara. *The Big Book of Jobs*. Lincolnwood, Ill.: VGM Career Horizons, 1997.

Schwartz, Stuart and Craig Conley. *Being a Leader*. Mankato, Minn.: Capstone High/Low Books, 1998.

Useful Addresses

Canada WorkInfoNet
Room 2161
Asticou Training Centre
241 Boulevard Cite des Jeunes
Hull, Quebec K1A 0M7

Employment and Training Administration
200 Constitution Avenue NW
Room N-4700
Washington, DC 20210

Training Information Source, Inc.
1424 South Clayton Street
Suite 200
Denver, CO 80210

U.S. Department of Labor
Office of Public Affairs
200 Constitution Avenue NW
Room S-1032
Washington, DC 20210

Internet Sites

America's Job Bank
http://www.ajb.dni.us

Skills Most in Demand by Employers
http://www.utoronto.ca/career/skills.htm

The Training Information Source
http://www.training-info.com/

Index